The sky's the limit.

May you know
how loved you
are!

Celia Anne Whitler

New Beginnings

Words and Music for Graduates

Celia Whitler

ABINGDON PRESS
Nashville

NEW BEGINNINGS

This book is printed on acid-free paper.

ISBN 978-1-426-70027-9

09 10 11 12 13 14 15 16 17 18 – 10 9 8 7 6 5 4 3 2 1
PRINTED IN MEXICO

This book is dedicated to Celia Hallgren, who always had a dream and taught me never to stop believing, and to the wonder boys, Ron, Max, and Zach. I love you most!

For you, the reader: May the end of your beginning show you that love will lead the way.

Thanks to:
Photography shoot: Russ Rohrer, photographer; Kelly Green, hair and makeup; Dianna Maher, great house

The incredible production team: Susan, Billie, Anna, Marcia

The lyrics to "Love Will Lead the Way" are inside the pages of this book, along with selected Scriptures and a few of my thoughts about new beginnings, dreams, and love.

Enjoy the journey – Celia

Congratulations. You have made it this far, and you are beginning something new—entering uncharted territory. You are like an explorer. Around every bend is a new adventure. Expect wonderful things to happen, and at times know that you may have to make something happen! You are amazing, and you are loved just as you are; not how you will be one day. Remember that you will never be alone. May these words and these songs give you food for the journey.

I believe love will lead your way.

The end of your beginning
is where you are today.

Not that I have already obtained this or have already
reached the goal; but I press on to make it my own,
because Christ Jesus has made me his own.
— Philippians 3:12

Small miracles occur every day, and I believe
that when we forgive and are forgiven . . .

. . .we experience one of those miracles.

soul

heart

No small task to come this far,

You shall love the Lord your God with all your heart,
and with all your soul, and with all your strength, and
with all your mind; and your neighbor as yourself.

— Luke 10:27

mind

Each day we have to choose, over and over, the selflessness of love.

It's written on your face.

. . . you show that you are a letter of Christ, prepared by us, written not with ink but with the Spirit of the living God, not on tablets of stone but on tablets of human hearts.

— 2 Corinthians 3:3

Follow

Follow your heart. You are the only one who knows what's a match for you.
You are the only one who can make your passion and your dreams come true.

Your Heart

No one gets here all alone, and we're not here to stay.

Again Jesus spoke to them, saying, "I am the light of the world. Whoever follows me will never walk in darkness but will have the light of life."

— John 8:12

Who has been there for you?

As you go, remember this —

Do not let your hearts be troubled.
Believe in God, believe also in me.
— John 14:1

We are not alone, and we are loved just

as we are.

Love will lead.

O give thanks to the LORD, for he is good;
for his steadfast love endures forever.
— 1 Chronicles 16:34

Blessing

The real blessing is in the exchange: getting to know people, to love what

Face the sunrise, seize your day

Let me hear of your steadfast love in the morning,
    for in you I put my trust.
Teach me the way I should go,
    for to you I lift up my soul.

                     — Psalm 143:8

As we continue to take steps toward God's grace and wholeness, those places that were once filled with pain become places filled with joy and peace.

Joy

Peace

Trust tomorrow, don't be afraid.

Keep alert, stand firm in
your faith, be courageous,
be strong. Let all that you
do be done in love.
— 1 Corinthians 16:13-14

If fear wasn't a factor,
what dream would you pursue?

Hold on to truth,

We know that all things work together for good for those who love God, who are called according to his purpose.

— Romans 8:28

Chart a new course

Do you need to change some old habits, make some new friends, chart a new course?

Let go
of yesterday

. . . for we walk by
faith, not by sight.
— 2 Corinthians 5:7

Where do you see yourself
in five, ten, or twenty years?

Always have a dream —

Do not be conformed to this world, but be transformed by the renewing of your minds, so that you may discern what is the will of God —what is good and acceptable and perfect.

— Romans 12:2

Who inspires you?

Love will lead the way.

For where your treasure is, there your heart
will be also.

— Luke 12:34

Home is not a geographic place;
home is being surrounded with love.

From where you stand,
there are many roads to take

For surely I know the plans I have for you, says the
LORD, plans for your welfare and not for harm, to give
you a future with hope.

— Jeremiah 29:11

Christ travels with you.

From where you've been,

Do not worry about anything . . . let your requests be made known to God.

— Philippians 4:6

How will you
begin today to
give your all
to finding and
living out your
dreams?

You've dreamed of this place.

Don't let anyone look down on you because you are young, but set an example for the believers in speech, in life, in love, in faith and in purity.

— 1 Timothy 4:12, NIV

someday is today

Don't wait for "someday."
Who are you? What is
your uniqueness?

So take a step,
    and you will grow
        stronger each day.

. . . endurance produces character, and character
produces hope, and hope does not disappoint us,
because God's love has been poured into our hearts
through the Holy Spirit that has been given to us.

— Romans 5:4-5

What's the next step
you need to take?

Say a prayer,
remember this —

In your relationships with one
another, have the same attitude of
mind Christ Jesus had.
— Philippians 2:5, TNIV

live Christ

Share Christ every day,
be open, don't judge, love
others as Christ loves.

Love will lead.

Bear one another's burdens, and
in this way you will fulfill the law
of Christ.

— Galatians 6:2

We can be agents of God's miracles
    when we become selfless sharers.

Though all the voices around
      seem louder than the song,

So if anyone is in Christ,
there is a new creation:
everything old has passed
away; see, everything has
become new!
                  – 2 Corinthians 5:17

sing your song

The world is big enough to start over.
There's room to forgive yourself, to make new friends,
and to build a better life.

Believe in yourself ...

So I tell you, whatever you ask for in prayer, believe
that you have received it, and it will be yours.

— Mark 11:24

What is your story?

What have you learned that you cherish,
embrace, laugh at, or want to change?
Make space for something you love.

You'll have strength to carry on.

I can do all things through Christ who strengthens me.
— Philippians 4:13, NKJV

What if you took
an inventory of
your life to discover
what you might be
holding back?

Love will lead the way.

And now faith, hope, and love abide,
these three; and the greatest of these is love.
— 1 Corinthians 13:13

"We can do no great things,
only small things with great love."
– Mother Teresa

Love will lead the way.

Above all, clothe yourselves with love, which binds everything together in perfect harmony.
— Colossians 3:14

What's
the worst thing
that could happen if
you follow your passion?

You could fail or you could
lose your way, but you
might discover
yourself.

Wherever you are today, know that you are not alone. Others have stood where you stand and are cheering you on from the sidelines.

Whether your next step is a baby step or a large leap, we have all been there. Anyone who says they weren't scared of a new beginning, even a little scared about how or if it would work out, well, they just aren't being honest.

Breathe, pray, sit knee to knee with someone you trust and share your dreams and your fears. You are amazing, so believe in yourself and be the best you!

. . . in all these things we are more than conquerors through him who loved us. For I am convinced that neither death, nor life, nor angels, nor rulers, nor things present, nor things to come, nor powers, nor height, nor depth, nor anything else in all creation, will be able to separate us from the love of God in Christ Jesus our Lord.

— Romans 8:37-39

Live Christ

Love Christ

Share Christ

Be Christ

All these things do today

All these things along your way

"Be the change
   you wish to see."
                   – Gandhi

Love Will Lead the Way

The end of your beginning is where you are today.

No small task to come this far, it's written on your face.

No one gets here all alone, and we're not here to stay.

As you go, remember this—love will lead.

Face the sunrise, seize your day;

Trust tomorrow, don't be afraid.

Hold on to truth, let go of yesterday;

Always have a dream—love will lead the way.

From where you stand, there are many roads to take;
From where you've been, you've dreamed of this place.
So take a step, and you will grow stronger each day.
Say a prayer, remember this—love will lead.

Though the voices all around seem louder than the song,
Believe in yourself . . . you'll have the strength to carry on.

Love will lead the way.

The Best Is Yet to Come

All this time, I've wasted days.
I've heard all my life . . . "Just you wait."
Then one day I heard Your voice,
I let go and believed.

The best is yet to come, I'm looking toward tomorrow,
The gift of a new day . . . the blessings that will follow.
I'm trusting in Your word; I'm leaning on Your truth.
All along You knew the best was yet to come.

It's all clear.
God wants nothing less than each of us near,
And to live our best.
I've surrendered without warning . . . All I have and all I'm holding.

So when I'm in that place and each of us is some days . . .
Where hope is hard to see, seems the darkness covers me.
I will hold on to the Savior who came to save us.
Hold on to the Savior who came to save us.
Hold on.

All along You knew the best was yet to come.
Hold on, hold on to the Savior. Hold on.
The best is yet to come.

New Beginnings

Words and Music for Graduates

1. Love Will Lead the Way
2. The Best Is Yet to Come
3. Live Christ

Produced by Celia & Ron Whitler
Mixed by Brent Maher
© 2008 Celia & Ron Whitler
Dog Not Included/ASCAP

www.celiamusic.net

Recording team, in order of appearance:

Celia Whitler, Vocals

Thad Beaty, Acoustic Guitar

Jason Collum, Drums

Mark Childers, Bass

Chance Scoggins and Michelle Swift, Background Vocals

Ilya Toshinsky, Guitars and other Stringed Instruments

Charles Yingling, Recording Engineer

Brent Maher, Mixing

Ken Love, Mastering